WEATHER AND CLIMATE THROUGH INFOGRAPHICS

Rebecca Rowell

graphics by
Venitia Dean

Lerner Publications Company
Minneapolis

Lerner Publications Company
A division of Lerner Publishing Group, Inc.
241 First Avenue North
Minneapolis, MN U.S.A. 55401

Website address: www.lernerbooks.com

Main text set in Univers LT Std 12/15.
Typeface provided by Adobe Systems.

Library of Congress Cataloging-in-Publication Data
Rowell, Rebecca.
    Weather and climate through infographics / by Rebecca Rowell.
      p.   cm. — (Super science infographics)
    Includes index.
    ISBN 978–1–4677–1292–7 (lib. bdg. : alk. paper)
    ISBN 978–1–4677–1790–8 (eBook)
    1. Weather—Juvenile literature. 2. Climatology—Juvenile literature. I. Title.
QC981.3.R675 2014
551.6—dc23   2013004785

Manufactured in the United States of America
1 – BP – 7/15/13

CONTENTS

THE WONDERS OF WEATHER AND CLIMATE

Do you have a future that includes all things weather and climate? To find out, take this test.

1. **Do you want to know what causes the seasons?**

2. **Do you enjoy discovering record temperatures?**

3. **Are you curious about clouds?**

4. **Do you have extreme interest in extreme weather?**

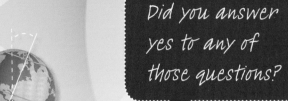

Did you answer yes to any of those questions?

CONGRATULATIONS!

You've got the right stuff to explore the wonders of meteorology and climatology. Earth's weather and climates are complex and diverse. They involve the sun, Earth's location and rotation, the sky, and water.

Meteorologists and climatologists use graphs, charts, and other infographics to help sort through all the information. These same tools can help you understand what makes our planet a cool place—and a hot one too. The forecast looks good for learning. So read on to learn more about the interesting—and sometimes dangerous—features of weather and climate.

SAME DIFFERENCE: WEATHER VERSUS CLIMATE

Weather and climate are similar but not the same. Weather is what's going on in Earth's atmosphere at a particular place during a brief period of time, such as a day, a week, or a season. You know, temperature, cloudiness, precipitation, and wind. Climate is weather over a much longer period—usually 30 years. It lets you know what weather is usually like in a place.

The planet has a lot of climates. The categories are based on temperature, precipitation, and vegetation.

Very warm all year long and a lot of rain—the monthly average temperature throughout the year is above 64°F (18°C).

Very little precipitation—the ground can lose moisture because so little comes from the sky.

CLIMATE KEY

TYPE A	TYPE B	TYPE C
Tropical humid	Dry	Moist with mild winters

Warm summers, cold winters—the average temperature of the warmest month is above 50°F (10°C) and the coldest month is below 27°F (−3°C).

Warm summers, mild winters—the average temperature for the coldest month is 27°F to 64°F (−3°C to 18°C).

Mountainous climates affected by altitude. They can range from tropical to frigid.

Cold all year long—the average temperature of the warmest month is below 50°F (10°C).

TYPE D

Moist with cold winters

TYPE E

Polar

TYPE H

Highland

HERE COMES THE SUN

The sun releases lots and lots of energy. Very little of it reaches Earth, but enough gets here to light and heat the planet. This energy also causes the weather and affects climate.

MILLIONS OF MILES IN MINUTES

The sun's heat travels the 93 million miles (150 million kilometers) to Earth in approximately eight minutes.

BRING ON THE SUN

The sun shines on every place on Earth at least part of the year.

SERIOUS SUN POWER

Imagine a bridge made of ice that's 2 miles (3.2 km) wide, 1 mile (1.6 km) thick, and made of ice that's 2 miles (3.2 km) wide, 1 mile sun releases so much energy it would melt that bridge in one second.

8

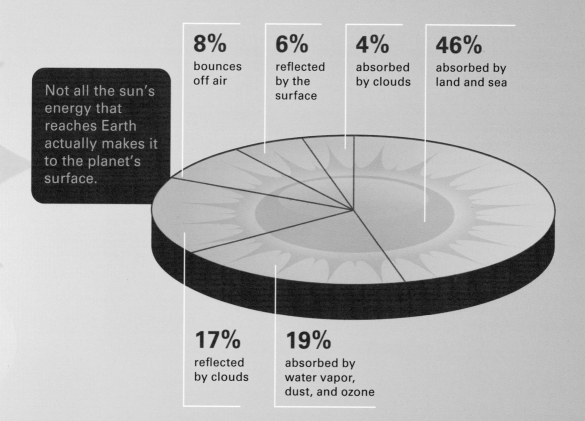

8%
bounces
off air

6%
reflected
by the
surface

4%
absorbed
by clouds

46%
absorbed by
land and sea

Not all the sun's energy that reaches Earth actually makes it to the planet's surface.

17%
reflected
by clouds

19%
absorbed by
water vapor,
dust, and ozone

ANGLE OF INCIDENCE

The sun's energy hits Earth with different intensities because the planet is round. Sunlight is most concentrated at the equator, where it hits the planet directly. Moving toward the poles, sunlight covers more area but is less concentrated. This difference in heating affects the climates and weather. The angle formed where sunlight hits the planet's surface is the angle of incidence.

THE SCOOP ON SEASONS

Some climates have distinct seasons that are very different from one another. Others don't. The equator is pretty much the same all year long, varying only in amount of rain. The farther you move from the equator, the more difference you'll see in the seasons.

This variety is a result of the sun and of Earth's orientation to it. Earth spins on an axis at an angle and orbits the sun. As the planet moves around the sun, the quantity of sunlight reaching different parts of Earth varies. The amount of variance throughout the year differs across the globe.

June 20 or 21: First day of summer in the Northern Hemisphere and winter in the Southern Hemisphere. The sun is farthest north from the equator.

There are 24 hours of light at the Arctic Circle.

Earth moves counterclockwise around the sun.

23.4°

March 20 or 21: First day of spring in the Northern Hemisphere and fall in the Southern Hemisphere

Earth circles the sun, but its orbit isn't actually a circle. It's an ellipse, which means it's shaped like an oval.

There are 24 hours of darkness at the Arctic Circle.

Earth rotates counterclockwise.

December 21 or 22: First day of winter in the Northern Hemisphere and spring in the Southern Hemisphere. The sun is farthest south from the equator.

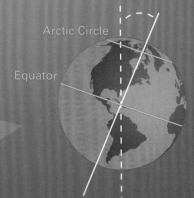

Arctic Circle

Equator

September 22 or 23: First day of fall in the Northern Hemisphere and spring in the Southern Hemisphere

The first day of spring and fall are the equinoxes. Day and night are the same length on these days.

RED HOT, ICE COLD

Do you like extremes? Earth experiences temperatures from hot, hot, hot to super-duper cold—and everything in between. Some climates tend to be hot or cold. Others have a combination of temperatures, varying from very warm summers to frigid winters. And sometimes, extremes occur in an unbelievably short period of time, with temperatures changing drastically in a matter of hours rather than across months.

–129°F (–89°C)
Coldest temperature on record
Vostok, Antarctica
July 21, 1983

APPROXIMATELY –150°F (–101°C)
Coldest estimated windchill ever recorded
A remote weather station in Antarctica
July 4, 2003

TEMPERATURE SCALES

The United States uses the Fahrenheit scale. Most other countries use the Celsius scale, which is also called centigrade. Need to convert a temperature?

Here's how:
°F to °C: (°F – 32) x 5/9
°C to °F: (°C x 9/5) + 32

Celsius

80
70
60
40
30
20
10
0

155°F TO 160°F (68°C TO 71°C)
Hottest heat index ever recorded
Dhahran, Saudi Arabia
July 8, 2003

134°F (57°C)
Hottest temperature on record
Death Valley, California
July 10, 1913

180
160
140
120
100
80
60
40
20
0

Fahrenheit

WORLD-RECORD CHANGE

Loma, Montana, set a world record in 1972 with the biggest temperature change in a 24-hour period. From January 14 to 15, the temperature went from −54°F to 49°F (−48°C to 9°C). That's 103 degrees!

EXTREME HEAT IN AUSTRALIA

In January 2013, temperatures in Australia were so high that the nation's meteorology bureau added two new colors to its weather charts. Dark purple and violet represent temperatures ranging from 124°F to 129°F (51°C to 54°C).

UP ABOVE THE WORLD SO HIGH

Do you ever look at the sky and wonder about it? There's a lot going on up there. What we usually call the sky is the atmosphere. It's a thin layer of air that surrounds the planet and acts like a protective bubble.

Earth's atmosphere is the most complex in the Milky Way. It provides the air we breathe, holds moisture, keeps in heat, and blocks damaging sunlight. The atmosphere extends for thousands of miles and gets thinner as you go farther away from the planet.

OUR CHILLY MOON

Earth's average surface temperature is 59°F (15°C). The moon's is 0°F (−18°C). The moon, unlike Earth, doesn't have an atmosphere to trap heat.

Exosphere: 375 to 6,200 miles (604 to 10,000 km) high
Atoms and molecules here escape into space.

Thermosphere: 56 to 375 miles (90 to 604 km) high
This layer can reach temperatures of up to 3,600°F (2,000°C).

Mesosphere: 31 to 56 miles (50 to 90 km) high
The coldest parts of the atmosphere are here—as low as −184°F (−120°C).

Stratosphere: 12 to 31 miles (20 to 50 km) high
The ozone is here. It soaks up the sun's ultraviolet rays, which are harmful.

Troposphere: Earth's surface to 4 to 12 miles (6 to 20 km) high

The air gets thinner the farther you go from Earth.

10 STEPS TO WATERING THE EARTH

Jumping in puddles in the rain can be fun. So can catching snowflakes on your tongue. These activities are made possible by precipitation. You know, water. More than half of Earth is covered in water, approximately 70 percent. That includes all forms: liquid, ice, and vapor. Most of it is in oceans. Water constantly moves through Earth and the atmosphere through the water cycle.

Rain is the most common form of precipitation.

Precipitation comes in many forms. The type is determined by temperature and size. Earth is the only known planet where water exists as a liquid, a solid, and a gas.

RAIN
0.02+ inches (0.5+ millimeters)

DRIZZLE
less than 0.02 inches

FREEZING RAIN

HAIL
0.2 inches or more

SLEET
0.2 inches or less

SNOW

1. **Evaporation**: The sun's heat changes water from liquid to vapor. It moves from Earth's surface into the air.

2. **Transpiration**: Water evaporates from trees and plants.

3. **Sublimation**: Ice and snow become water vapor, skipping the liquid phase.

4. **Condensation**: Water vapor changes back into liquid. Clouds form.

5. **Transportation**: Water moves in all states. This moves water from over the ocean to over land.

6. **Precipitation**: Water that falls to the earth. It occurs mostly as rain but includes snow.

7. **Runoff**: How water travels over the earth. It comes from rain and snow.

8. **Infiltration**: Water moves from the surface into the ground.

9. **Groundwater flow**: Water moves underground.

10. **Plant uptake**: Water moves from groundwater into soil, where plant and tree roots can get it.

THICK, THIN, PUFFY, WISPY

Stretching out on the ground and looking up at the clouds for familiar shapes can be a lot of fun. Clouds can be wispy and barely there or thick and fluffy. Sometimes, they stretch high into the atmosphere or blanket the sky.

Clouds form when so much moisture is in the air that vapor becomes water droplets or ice crystals. This happens when rising moist air is cooled enough to cause condensation or the amount of water in the air has increased, such as through evaporation. Check out the different cloud types and their shapes.

STRATUS
Forms at low levels and often covers the entire sky. *Stratus* is Latin for "layer."

FOG
A cloud at Earth's surface.

CIRRUS, NIMBUS, CUMULUS, STRATUS
Meteorologists categorize clouds by their height in the atmosphere and how they appear from below. These funny-sounding words are categories of clouds.

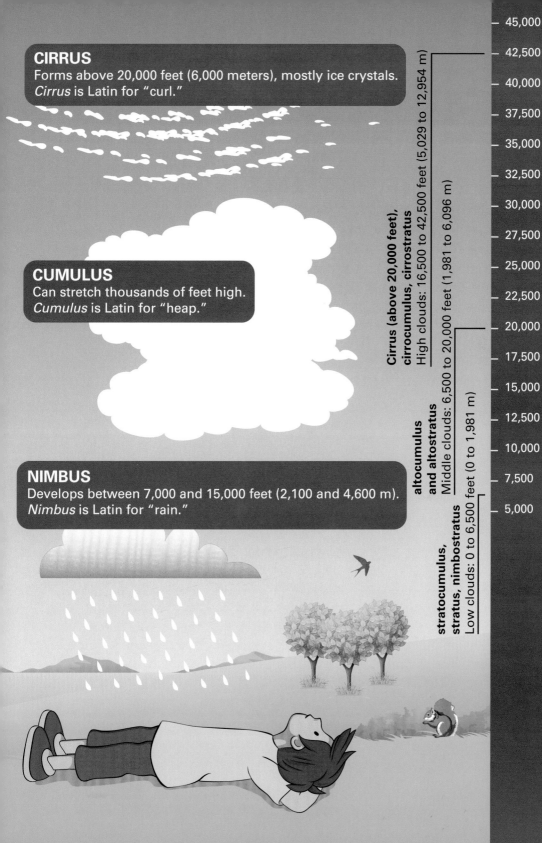

CIRRUS
Forms above 20,000 feet (6,000 meters), mostly ice crystals. *Cirrus* is Latin for "curl."

CUMULUS
Can stretch thousands of feet high. *Cumulus* is Latin for "heap."

NIMBUS
Develops between 7,000 and 15,000 feet (2,100 and 4,600 m). *Nimbus* is Latin for "rain."

Cirrus (above 20,000 feet), cirrocumulus, cirrostratus
High clouds: 16,500 to 42,500 feet (5,029 to 12,954 m)

altocumulus and altostratus
Middle clouds: 6,500 to 20,000 feet (1,981 to 6,096 m)

stratocumulus, stratus, nimbostratus
Low clouds: 0 to 6,500 feet (0 to 1,981 m)

cumulonimbus
Extends through all three levels

45,000
42,500
40,000
37,500
35,000
32,500
30,000
27,500
25,000
22,500
20,000
17,500
15,000
12,500
10,000
7,500
5,000

BLOW, WIND, BLOW

Ever wonder where wind comes from? It's air in motion. Heat differences cause air to move. Earth's atmosphere is in constant motion as warm air at the equator heads to the poles and cold air at the poles moves back to the equator. These shifts create global patterns of circulation and powerful jet streams high in the atmosphere—even winds capable of great destruction at Earth's surface.

THE DOLDRUMS
The area around the equator is often called the doldrums. Calm winds here make it difficult for weather.

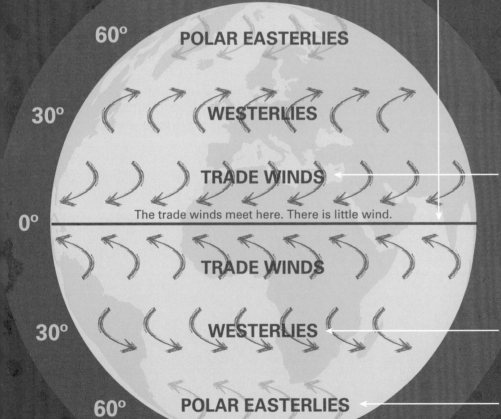

60° POLAR EASTERLIES

30° WESTERLIES

TRADE WINDS

The trade winds meet here. There is little wind.

0°

TRADE WINDS

30° WESTERLIES

60° POLAR EASTERLIES

Warm, steady breezes that blow westward and toward the equator.

Winds between 30° and 60° latitudes that blow from the west and toward the poles.

Winds above 60° latitude that blows over the poles from the east.

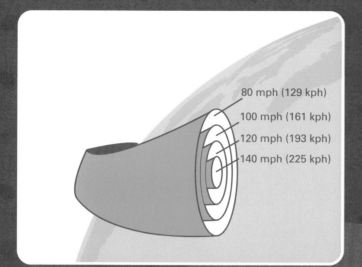

80 mph (129 kph)
100 mph (161 kph)
120 mph (193 kph)
140 mph (225 kph)

JET STREAMS

Each hemisphere often has two jet streams and sometimes three. Winds here blow at high speeds from west to east in long, narrow areas. Jet streams circle Earth in winding paths that change with the seasons. They're closer to the equator and move faster in winter than in summer. Some jet streams can cause storms. Others occur with nice weather.

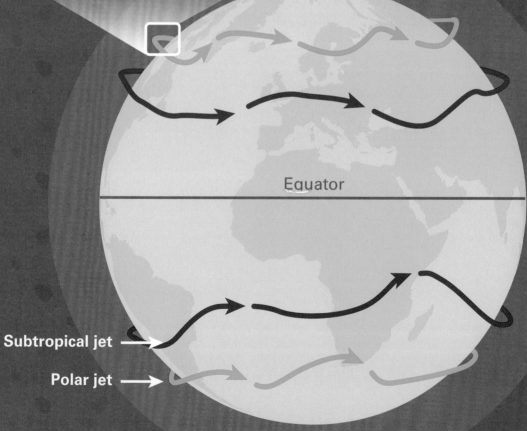

Equator

Subtropical jet ——→

Polar jet ——→

ROUND AND ROUND IT GOES

Earth's ocean water is like its atmosphere: constantly on the go, circling the globe. Ocean water moves heat from the equator to the poles at the surface and deep underwater. Ocean currents move water at the surface. And thermohaline circulation moves water far below the surface. The deep currents are slower than the surface currents. Changes in ocean temperature can cause major weather events, such as hurricanes and droughts.

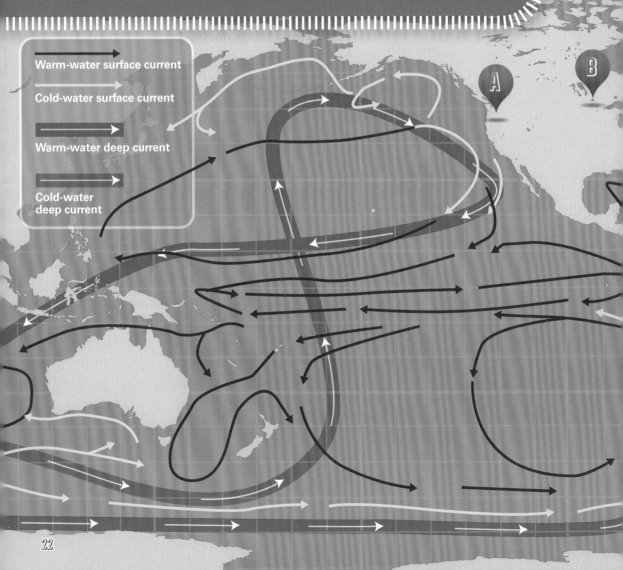

Warm-water surface current

Cold-water surface current

Warm-water deep current

Cold-water
deep current

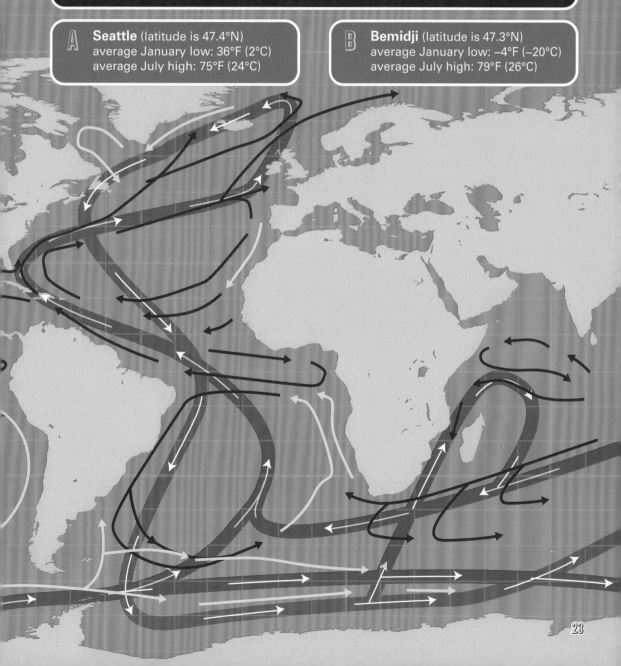

OCEAN AFFECTS TEMPERATURE

Land near water is more temperate than land far from water. That's because water changes temperature slowly. Coastal cities are warmed and cooled by winds blowing from the ocean. Winds that blow inland don't come directly from the ocean. Compare Seattle, Washington, and Bemidji, Minnesota. They're almost the same distance from the equator, but they have different climates. Winds blowing in from the ocean keep Seattle relatively cool in summer and warm in winter. Bemidji isn't near an ocean, so its summer and winter temperatures are more extreme.

A **Seattle** (latitude is 47.4°N)
average January low: 36°F (2°C)
average July high: 75°F (24°C)

B **Bemidji** (latitude is 47.3°N)
average January low: –4°F (–20°C)
average July high: 79°F (26°C)

FRONT AND CENTER

Air masses are major players in weather—because of their size and their effects. An air mass is a big body of air with similar temperature and moisture. An air mass can stretch for miles. Air masses form when air sits over an area long enough to match the area's temperature and moisture.

Air masses have boundaries called fronts. A warm air mass is led by a warm front. A cold air mass has a cold front. Fronts often cause changes in wind, humidity, cloudiness, and precipitation. While the different types of masses and fronts move differently, one thing is similar about them: the weather's going to change.

FRONTS ON A WEATHER MAP

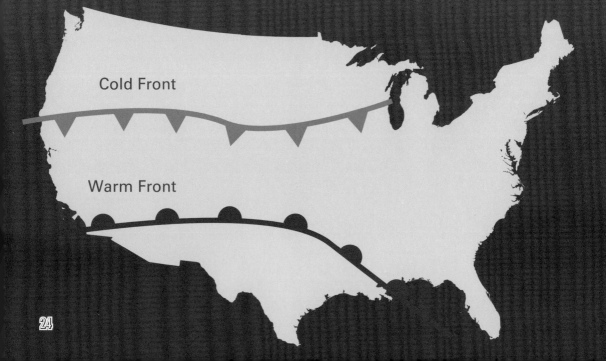

Cold Front

Warm Front

TYPES OF FRONTS

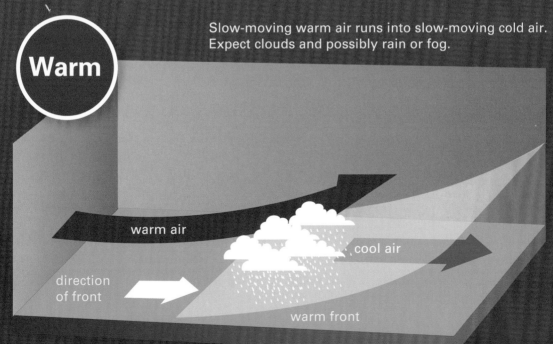

Cold

Fast-moving cold air runs into slow-moving warm air. Expect strong winds and thunderstorms.

warm air

cool air

direction of front

cold front

Cold fronts usually move faster than warm fronts.

Warm

Slow-moving warm air runs into slow-moving cold air. Expect clouds and possibly rain or fog.

warm air

cool air

direction of front

warm front

GOING EXTREME

Every year, people around the globe experience severe weather disasters. A single event can cause hundreds or even thousands of people to die or become homeless. Cleaning up and repairing what's left after an event can cost millions and millions of dollars. And recovery can take years.

1989
SATURIA-MANIKGANJ SADAR TORNADO

Manikganj District,
Bangladesh
April 26

About 1,300 people died, and tens of thousands were left homeless. It is believed to be the deadliest tornado in recorded history.

1995
MAYFEST STORM

Tarrant and Dallas
Counties, Texas
May 5

Twenty people died, dozens were injured, and damages were estimated at $2 billion.

1972
IRAN BLIZZARD

Iran
February

About 4,000 people died.

1970 1972 1973 1974 1975 1976 1977 1978 1979 1980 1981 1982 1983 1984 1985 1986

BLIZZARD

A severe winter storm with winds at least 35 mph (56 kph) for three hours and visibility limited to 0.25 miles (0.4 km).

TORNADO

Usually associated with thunderstorms, this is a destructive column of air that rotates and touches the ground and can have wind speeds as high as 300 mph (483 kph).

THUNDERSTORM

A violent storm with lightning, thunder, heavy rain, winds at least 58 mph (93 kph), and hail with a diameter of at least 0.75 in (2 cm).

2005
HURRICANE KATRINA

Gulf Coast of the
United States
August

Almost 2,000 people were
killed. Katrina, the most
expensive hurricane in U.S.
history, caused $80 billion
in damage.

2003
EUROPEAN HEAT WAVE

Europe
June to mid-August

At least 30,000 people died.
The heat wave melted
glaciers, contributed to rock
slides and forest fires, and
affected harvests.

1999
VENEZUELA FLOODS

Caracas, Venezuela
December

Two weeks of heavy rain
caused flooding and
landslides. It is estimated that
10,000 to 30,000 people were
killed, and tens of thousands
were made homeless.

87 1988 1989 1990 1991 1992 1993 1994 1995 1996 1997 1998 1999 2000 2001 2002 2003 2004 2005

HURRICANE

A strong, circular storm that
starts over warm, tropical
oceans, with winds at least
74 mph (119 kph) and lots of
rain. It causes storm surge,
making sea levels reach
higher than usual—as much
as 20 feet (6 m). Hurricanes
are usually 200 miles (320
km) across. They're also
known as cyclones, tropical
cyclones, and typhoons.

DROUGHT

A lack of rain for a long
period that leads to water
shortages, damages crops,
reduces flow of streams,
and dries out the ground.

FLOODS AND FLASH FLOODS

An overflowing of a river,
sometimes seasonally,
sometimes because of storm
surge. Flash floods occur
suddenly, within six hours of
heavy rain, and can take
over streets.

FROM OUTSIDE TO YOU

Weather information is in high demand. The National Weather Service (NWS) gathers weather data from high and low and feeds it into supercomputers that turn it into forecasts. These weather predictions go to all kinds of organizations and often shape predictions published in all kinds of places. Entire television and cable stations are devoted to weather. Here's the process—it's as easy as 1-2-3.

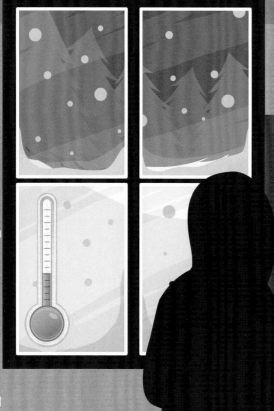

WEATHER WATCHERS

The NWS has almost 290,000 volunteers trained to spot severe weather. In free classes, spotters learn about identifying and reporting severe weather, as well as severe weather safety.

STEP 1: GATHER DATA

Meteorologists gather information from a variety of sources to create the most accurate forecast possible. The information includes measurements of things such as temperature, wind direction, wind speed, humidity, and liquid precipitation (like rain or snow).

STEP 2: PROCESS DATA

Supercomputers process weather observations and make predictions. The National Weather Service runs these computers in the United States.

STEP 3: CREATE AND DISTRIBUTE FORECASTS

The NWS has a variety of offices and centers that distribute forecasts and warnings. Other groups and people create and share forecasts, including private forecasting companies and television meteorologists. The military has forecasters too.

Glossary

ALTITUDE: the height of something in the sky. Clouds are classified by altitude.

ANGLE OF INCIDENCE: the angle formed by sunlight when it hits Earth. The angle of incidence varies from place to place on Earth.

ATMOSPHERE: the sky. Earth's atmosphere is complex and protects the planet.

AXIS: a straight line through an object around which it spins. Earth's axis stretches from the North Pole to the South Pole.

BLIZZARD: a severe snowstorm. Blizzards have strong winds of at least 35 mph (56 kph) per hour.

CLIMATE: the pattern of weather at a specific location over a long period of time, usually 30 years. Earth has several climates.

CLOUD: a collection of water droplets or ice crystals in the sky. Clouds exist at different heights and take different shapes.

CURRENT: an area of air or water that moves faster than the area around it. Ocean currents move water from the equator to the poles and back again.

ELLIPSE: an oval. Earth's orbit around the sun is an ellipse.

METEOROLOGY: the study of the atmosphere, particularly weather

ORBIT: a path one object repeats regularly around another object. Earth orbits the sun.

PRECIPITATION: any form of water that falls from the sky and reaches the ground. Rain, drizzle, and snow are types of precipitation.

THERMOHALINE CIRCULATION: a deep ocean conveyor belt. Thermohaline circulation moves water from the equator to the poles.

WATER CYCLE: the series of steps water takes as it moves from the ground, to the air, and back to the ground. In the water cycle, water exists as vapor, liquid, and solid.

WEATHER: what the atmosphere is doing at a specific place during a specific, short period of time. Weather includes temperature, precipitation, cloudiness, and wind.

Further Information

Curiosity: Climate and Weather
http://dsc.discovery.com/tv-shows
/curiosity/topics/climate-weather.htm
Investigate topics of climate and
weather through a variety of online
videos, covering topics such as the
relationship between oceans and
climate and how the sun's behavior
may affect Earth's climates.

Fleisher, Paul. *Doppler Radar,
Satellites, and Computer Models:
The Science of Weather Forecasting.*
Minneapolis: Lerner Publications,
2010.
Check out the tricky science of
weather forecasting, including the
tools meteorologists use.

Fleisher, Paul. *Gases, Pressure,
and Wind: The Science of the
Atmosphere.* Minneapolis: Lerner
Publications, 2010.
Investigate the many facets of the
atmosphere in this colorful book.

Fleisher, Paul. *Lightning, Hurricanes,
and Blizzards: The Science of
Storms.* Minneapolis: Lerner
Publications, 2010.
Extreme weather enthusiasts will
enjoy learning how and where
storms form and other interesting
facts.

Hynes, Margaret. *Extreme Weather.*
New York: Macmillan, 2011.
Explore the extremes of Earth's
weather in this book. Photos and
illustrations help tell the story.

Kids' Crossing
http://www.eo.ucar.edu/kids/index
.html
This website has all kinds of weather
and climate information. It includes
games and activities, plus links to
explore. The site was created by the
National Center for Atmospheric
Research and the University
Corporation for Atmospheric
Research.

Understanding Weather Patterns
http://www.nc-climate.ncsu.edu
/edu/k12/WeatherPatterns
Learn more about the weather
patterns that affect us every day.
This site by the University of North
Carolina is designed for students in
kindergarten through high school.

Weather
http://www.edheads.org/activities
/weather/index.shtml
This online, interactive animation
has information about predicting
and reporting weather.

Weather Channel Kids!
http://theweatherchannelkids.com
Explore a variety of weather topics
at this site by the Weather Channel.
Learn about climate and careers
in meteorology or play weather
games.

LERNER

SOURCE™

Expand learning beyond the printed book. Download free, complementary
educational resources for this book from our website, www.lernersource.com.

Index